Paracosm
A POETRY COLLECTION

emma the poet

PARACOSM

Copyright © 2023 emma the poet
All rights reserved.
ISBN: 9798861432993

PARACOSM

PARACOSM

PARACOSM

Would you walk with me
To the edge of my world
To the ledge of my mind
When the weight of circumstance
Society
And time
All become a little too much to handle

And right now
I have nothing left in me to offer
Other than a sigh of defeat
Followed by a few tears

I know that in the end
Everything will be fine
But would you sit with me
Just for a little while
Until the pain of this moment subsides

***

PARACOSM

On the days I feel empty
And hopelessly alone
I take a walk below the trees
And dream of life's possibilities

A dream of loving you
Of quitting a job that brings tears to my eyes
Of laughing with friends on the beach below a full moon

A dream of writing more
Of baking more
Of living more

I live a life of daydreams
Lost in the woods where cell phone notifications
Can't bring me back to earth

I am grounded in delusions
Of what could be
Because this reality leaves me feeling empty
Desperate and longing for something more
More kindness
More patience
More self-confidence
More love

And until that day comes
I'll sit below the trees
Daydreaming while tears roll down my cheeks

***

PARACOSM

Why do the flowers return each summer
When they know September winds
Will wilt away their carefree days

They must know the secrets
Of what makes this life worthwhile
To bloom in spite of ever-changing skies

***

PARACOSM

I drove past a row of red brick apartment buildings
With tall thin windows
Iron balconies
And ivy wrapping around the fire escape

Suddenly a life I had once thought would be mine
Raced through my mind
I saw the parties I would have had in the living room
With friends I have not met
The rainy days spent next to the window sill
Watching a drizzly street full of people
Rushing around to get to some more important place

It's strange
That at one time in my life
I was on track to live in one of those studios
Or at least one just like it
In some city with some job
That I would have sworn I loved
Or maybe I would have chased that dream
To become someone inspiring
Someone worth remembering

And yet the choices I made
Derailed destiny's train
And here I am
In my car
Driving to a home in the town I thought I'd never see again
A place where I spend nights under stars
Dreaming of what could have been
A place where longing hides behind every corner
But love lives in every room

PARACOSM

Are we nothing more
Than the sum of the choices we choose
Is reality an option
Or is there something outside ourselves
That leads us to the people and places
Meant for us to find

***

PARACOSM

I dream of sweet Sunday afternoons
Spent in sunshine
Lying on soft linens
Laughing next to you

***

PARACOSM

Sometimes I look in the mirror and see
A girl staring back who isn't me
She looks young
And tired
And sad
Though I am most certainly all of those things too
This stranger in the mirror
Has a hopelessness behind her eyes
That couldn't be mine

***

PARACOSM

Let's run away to the sky
Or get lost in the breeze
Fall asleep with the stars
And then dance in the trees

We'll find the softest place
This world has to lie
And spend the rest of our days
Free from the tears in our eyes

***

PARACOSM

The autumn fog fell below
The weeping willow tree
As if to hide her tears
From a world who couldn't understand
The grief that walks hand in hand
With letting go of everything that you are
And to rest for a while below a rosy sunrise
Until the songs of spring return once more

***

PARACOSM

I took an afternoon nap
On a pile of fresh laundry
My sheets tumbled in the dryer
And I knew I should wait
Until I could lay them across my bed
But the smell of clean cotton
Is as good as melatonin
And nothing is as inviting
As warm clothes on soft carpet
On a Sunday afternoon

***

PARACOSM

Sometimes
There are days when it is okay
To admit that nothing feels right
And you'd rather be anywhere
Than where you are right now
And be anyone but you

Sometimes
It is okay
To get lost in dreams
Of all that could never be

***

PARACOSM

How lovely to be alive on this golden October night
The air feels cleaner somehow
And your cheeks glow pink below these amber leaves

I wish I could stay in this moment forever
The only touch softer than this flannel
Is your hand in mine

I wonder how the trees let go of all that they are
So gracefully
In a gentle blush of color across the sky
They release control of everything they have
To the autumn breeze

I could learn a few lessons from these Pennsylvania woods
Like accepting that you may or may not
Dream of a life forever spent with me
And that by letting go of control
Means there is hope for a heavenly spring

***

PARACOSM

I know that sorrow haunts the hollows of your mind
And lately all you feel is empty inside
I know it in my bones
And I wish that you wouldn't cry alone

We share smiles and sweet imaginings
Of all the wonderful dreams that could one day be
We laugh at jokes
That only make sense in each other's company

Why can't we let our lips tremble
Let tears roll down our cheeks
It's as if breaking down together
Would bring an end to our soft symphony

When I feel alone on my darkest days
All I can think about
Is how desperately I want to run to you
And hope that you can make out what is wrong
Between my incoherent sobs

But when you lock your garden gate
On nights when you question your worth
And your place in this world
When all your dreams start to fall apart

It makes me feel like I am wrong in my want
To lean on your shoulder when my head won't stay up
And that my history of extending my hand
When you were on the ground
Must have done more harm for your feelings than good

PARACOSM

Maybe one day
A day that I hope comes very soon
We will hear each other's cries to the moon
And we can sit with each other on the nights
When terrifying thoughts fill our minds

***

PARACOSM

I am not made of jade
And my scars do not sparkle with gold
I am not stronger
Because of the pain that left marks on my soul
I am an ordinary human
Made of flesh and bone
I bleed when I am cut
And I shattered when you threw your stones

***

I worry because life isn't promised and I know it
I don't want to take a moment for granted
And I want it all
Right now
A wonderful and wondrous life

I am impatient
Because I know that the countdown has already begun
And I haven't had the chance to figure out what I want
I only have one shot
I am not anxious because I hate life
But because I want to love it right

***

PARACOSM

I have eyes full of stars
And a longing for something more
If you'd have me
I'll take you by the hand
And you can chase these dreams with me
But you have to want it too
This fantastical life of wonder
Because I simply cannot choose
Between loving what could be
And you

***

PARACOSM

Why do I silence my joy
When you ask me about my day
And I say *it was just okay*
But what I really mean
Is that I went on a walk so beautiful
My soul started to sing
I drank iced tea with my bagel
And thought to myself
This moment is reason enough for living

But it's not just the light in my life
That I hide with vague words like *fine* and *alright*
When I tell you that I'm feeling down
I really mean
The tears that fell from my eyes
Two hours before we met for coffee still sting
And the weight of existence
Feels like eternal suffering

I can't set the heaviness of my feelings
Onto your shoulders
Because lovely or melancholy
My emotions rip me apart to the very core of my heart
And I am scared that you will minimize
What it means for me to feel deeply
Passionately
Melodramatically

PARACOSM

I love the moments that feel overwhelmingly wonderful
The moments that feel like daydreams
And I also love that anxiety and pain
Means that I cared a lot about the people I love
And the opportunities I lost
I love these feelings
Even when I sometimes feel
Like I am trapped in a nightmare

Maybe I should be more worried
About the effects of these emotions
Or maybe having feelings this heavy
Is simply what it means to be alive fully

***

PARACOSM

I do not wince in the rain
My face has grown used to
Tears that stain my face
And the sting of an afternoon sun
Is nothing compared to the pain
Of desperation

***

PARACOSM

I love this little town
I promise that I do
I love how we laugh our way down Main Street at midnight
And leave our cars unlocked without worry or fear
I love the ice cream shop and walks through the park
And how maple trees line every street
I love late nights at the county fair every summer
And going to the same farm for pumpkins every Halloween

It's just that I can't help but believe
There is more out there for me to see
If you want to
You can come with me

But when I shared these dreams
A look of empty anger washed over your face
And all you could say was

Unpack the car
You're breaking my heart
Why do you feel like you have to go so far

You'll just get lost on city streets
Chasing a dream that will never be
People like you and me
Don't become someone
Who smiles to crowds through the tv

Let's go down to the bar
And keep wishing on stars to fill this void in our hearts
You think you have to go someplace far
To live a life worth remembering
Then what does that mean for me and my dreams
The hopes that I let fade after turning eighteen

PARACOSM

Go on and run from this place
You'll be back in six months
When the real world knocks you on your face

But that's okay
I'll be here waiting
And we can drive the car down to the park
Swing after dusk below shooting stars
And find a solemn sense of content
To patch our broken hearts

You know you might find a way to feel happy
If you can try to make peace
With the life we have been given
Don't get angry at me
It's just way things are supposed to be

***

PARACOSM

And this sadness I feel
Is the kind that hollows out your chest
Until there is nothing left

***

PARACOSM

When I dream about
The life I wish
I could make for myself
My eyes are overcome with grief

Because the small home
Full of light
And tea
And blankets
And wildflowers
Is not an unreasonable fantasy

Neither is laughing with friends
Or waking up next to someone who loves me
Or an occasional trip to the sea

But the universe has decided
That this is all too much for me

That this soft little life
Will always be a dream

***

PARACOSM

I saw my entire life with you
Late nights that turned into breakfast
Parties and city lights
Walks below a sunny sky
Quiet time after bad news
Holding hands when there is nothing else to cling to

I said that I wanted to cry all my tears next to you
And you said nothing at all
A silence that shattered my heart
After I gave everything to you

Then you said I'd be better off
With someone who could love me
In all the ways you had once wanted to

But that would be wrong
Even if I could find a way to move on
I'd look in his eyes and think about
How it should be you
Firing off jokes over radio tunes
That we once danced to
On summer nights
Dozing off by a fireside

I wanted this dreamy phase to last forever
Maybe if I had realized
It was okay to love you sooner
We'd be sleeping tonight
Under starlight
Next to each other

***

PARACOSM

How do you manifest
The life you live in your dreams
When raised expectations
Hurt worse than feeling empty

***

PARACOSM

I didn't fall from grace
I jumped
A smile across my face
With the assumption you would
Catch me
Not let me
Crash land without my wings
You left me in pieces
A fragment of who I used to be
You told me
No-
Scolded me
That my dreams were delusions
The life I had once believed
Could be reality

***

PARACOSM

What image do you see in your daydreams
Is it me
Because I fantasize taking your time
And I guess I just want you to want mine

***

PARACOSM

Displaced from a life I had hoped to love
What happens when you change your dreams
When you come to terms with your reality
And the watered-down version of happiness
You learned to accept
Still cannot quench the desperate pleas
For something that feels extraordinary

You find a new fixation
A new fantasy
Build a new place to run
A place where you can hide away from your problems
Lower your expectations
Forget that dream of a dream
That light inside
The one that kept you holding on

***

PARACOSM

This life is too impossibly short
And too terrifyingly long
To pretend like I am okay
When I am so painfully not

***

PARACOSM

Maybe I expected too much from this life
From you

But I know that I would have found a way
To make any dream you found the courage to whisper in my ear
Come true

And I really thought
You would have done that for me too

***

PARACOSM

I feel myself slipping away again
I try to fight it
With vegetables
And peppermint tea
And walks in the autumn air

But I have let my garbage pile up again
I am unable to let go of the wrappers and crumbs
Hoping they might take the place
Of stolen dreams
And lost sleep

The tears won't stop again
Not for rush hour traffic
Or a warm dinner
Or even you

My head is so loud again
With every unkind word that has left me feeling hurt
And the memory of the ones
Who made me feel like I could never be enough

You see it's getting bad again
And I wish I knew
If one day the trouble of fighting
Will be worth all the tears I have been through

**

PARACOSM

It's not fair
And it's not divine
This is just life
And I hope you find
Moments of joy
In the storm that it is
To be alive

***

PARACOSM

How do I leave the life in my head
One where my cheeks are blushed
From wine I've never tried
At a dinner in the south of France
One where my legs are sore
From climbing dreamy desert mountains out west
One where my bones ache
From the chill of running below imaginary northern lights
One where my tongue is sticky
From syrup and pancakes
After a Sunday morning spent with you

I have lived my whole life
Confined within the same time zone lines
Because I have not found the courage
To abandon these questions in my mind
What if you run out of money
What if you have nothing to go back to
What if the people you don't even really like
Resent you for leaving them behind

I am okay with this life in my mind
Though I still long to see new and lovely skies
Because the laughs I have shared
With the people I met in all the places I have never went
Felt so real
And I know what it means to feel
Free
Dance under the starlight
While I hold your hand
Forever
Or at least until this daydream ends

***

PARACOSM

I'm sorry I wasn't a better friend
I didn't ignore your texts or pull away
Because you did anything wrong

I really didn't think you would care
Or even notice
If I was around or not

Because low self-esteem
Is eating away the confidence in me
I just didn't think I mattered that much to you

And I'm sorry
Because you mattered to me too

I wish that I could tell my old self
That friendship is a part of being alive
And people care a lot more than you think that they do
And they care about you

I'm sorry
I should have been a better friend to you

***

PARACOSM

I lie awake
Thinking of you
And I wonder
If you have ever lost sleep
Because of me too

***

PARACOSM

The sunlight hits the muddy November brush
And flashbacks rush through my mind
From a summer when I was still young enough
Not to know the pain of love

I am stuck in my past
Lost in days sweeter than these
A time when I really believed
That there was such a thing
As unconditional love
And that people would do kind things to fill an ache in me
Simply because I was in a moment of need
Not for glory or to have something to hang over my head

My cheeks start to flush
As I remember the Florida sun of my youth
It's almost as though this memory
Is the reason they are turning light pink
Not the frozen mountain air
Outside a house that never felt exactly like home

Salt streams down my face
And freezes below my nose
I try to think about all the kindness I have ever received
How can I let myself
Slip into such generalizing and dark thoughts
After just a few disappointing moments of desperation

When the truth is
That many people have given me plenty of love
And that when I find the strength to ask for help
Most of the time
People will come

***

PARACOSM

What do I do
When sorrow has seeped
Into every dream and
Memory of you

***

PARACOSM

How long can I get away with
Crying on my bedroom floor
How long until you tell me
You can't hold the weight of my sorrow anymore

People love a beautiful tragedy
A girl who looks lovely
While she falls apart gracefully

My silver tears will one day dry
Leaving wrinkles around my eyes
And those who once thought
Their love might be enough to help me
Will pass by and think

What a shame
What a waste of a pretty face

***

PARACOSM

I just wanted this life with you
Life in a world where nothing makes sense
Where the cruel get ahead
And the gentle are drowning in sorrow

I decided to face it with you
Because you reminded me that there is beauty
In the pain of humanity
And I wanted to hold onto your light

I wanted to laugh with you under shooting stars
Until the time turned into an hour
That we can't decide whether to call morning or night
Creeps up and sends us home

I wanted the chance to make you feel
Like more than an accidental blip in this galaxy
Take your hand when you feel lonely
And ask for a silent dance in the living room

I wanted to warm your home in December
And pick you wildflowers in June
I wanted to find new reasons to love this world
But I wanted that with you

***

PARACOSM

I have been waiting
For something to happen to me
A miracle or adventure
That would change my life for the better
Because I did not believe
That I had the ability to create beautiful things on my own

But no one is coming
There are no signs from above
A shooting star is just a star
The breeze on the back of my neck is just the wind
And the only way for me to change direction
Is to turn my own feet around
And learn to love the ground below

***

PARACOSM

When did these dreams become delusions
Of a life that could never be
How could I have blurred the lines
Between my mind and reality
And what if I don't want to let go
Of fantasies that keep me
From feeling so alone

***

PARACOSM

I miss me
I want to find myself again
That shamelessly loving girl
Who didn't care what bitter people thought
Who smiled without thinking about
Looking pretty in a picture
Or her crooked teeth

I miss the version of myself
Who carried a stack of card stock
With inspirational quotes in my purse
Just in case I stumbled across someone
In need of a gentle word

I miss the version of myself
That loved staying out late with my friends
Instead of anticipating an exhausting morning
Filled with disapproving words about
Priorities and what it takes to get ahead

I miss the version of myself
That truly believed in
Magic and dreams and adventurous things
I miss running through the forest
Without the weight of my worries
I miss the version of myself
Who was more concerned with loving fully
Than hiding in dreams

***

PARACOSM

And suddenly the heaviness was gone
I hadn't even realized it left
I just found myself
Singing along to the radio
While watching the trees on my way to work

And suddenly it had returned
I hadn't even realized it settled once more
I just found myself in silence
Unconcerned
For where I was or where I was going

And though this feeling rises and falls
With an unknown cause
Or antidote
I suspect eventually it will fade
As I learn to love more of each day

***

Tonight I'll stay up
Because I have missed the moon
And it reminds me of you

***

PARACOSM

When I look in your eyes
I see memories
Of the light we used to be
Sometimes when I cry at night
I wonder if it was all just a dream
But I remember those eyes
Under a star-lit sky
When you whispered
That you could never hurt me
An impossible promise
I somehow
Let you convince me you could keep
Now we sit together
Yet still alone
Love in irreparable pieces
At our feet

***

And at the end of the night
When I look up at the sky
I know it will all be alright

***

PARACOSM

It is okay if you didn't make your bed today
It is okay if you don't like green juice
Or running
Or waking up at 5 AM

Most people don't have 10 step skincare routines
Most people don't have 50 dollar travel mugs
Or Botox
Or Dyson Airwraps

It is normal to not have plans every weekend
It is normal to feel behind
Or lonely
Or mad

It is okay to want more for yourself
It is okay to make time to rest
Or create
Or dream

You are so much more
Than the sum of the things you don't have
You are not a self-improvement project
That never seems to end

You are doing the best you can
And you are enough

***

PARACOSM

I don't know how to bring up the heaviness
That lives in my head
How do you say
I am drowning below the current of my restless thoughts
During a casual conversation
Or in the middle of our comfortable silence

I wait for someone
To sit with me on the couch
And ask me to let my strength down
Beg me to release the secrets and reasons for my sadness

In this dream of gentle inquiries
Relief spills out and down my cheeks
A weight lifted from me
And even if my trusted listener cannot guarantee
That life will change for the better
And suddenly one day I will feel free
I will walk lighter knowing
That that someone really heard me

**

PARACOSM

Can we turn off the lights
Lie on the couch
And listen to the rain
Watch the lightning under soft blankets
And the trees sway below skies of grey

Maybe then I will feel safe enough
To whisper my secret insecurities
And you'll feel light enough to release
The pain that you usually keep quiet
Even though you have every right to scream

***

PARACOSM

I think about the times
I looked at the lines of your face
And how badly I wanted to tell you

About the dreams of walking
Through an endless garden
Where white flowers
Dangle from the sky forever

The dreams of dancing
At a stoplight in a midnight rain
While flashing city lights keep the beat
And your laugh echoes down the alley

The dreams of living
In a house with big windows
And soft carpet
And all your pictures hang on the walls

I wish I told you
I love you more

Because I thought I knew what they meant
When they tell you life changes fast

And now all I have
Are the memories of me
Never telling you
How much I love your laugh

***

PARACOSM

You threw a party
I wasn't invited to
And the whole night
I sat alone on my bedroom floor
Thinking about how I have become a secret that you keep
From your world and the people in it
I scheme in my head
About what you might be doing
Or saying
And why you wouldn't be able to see
How hurt I might be

Is there a word for having a nightmare
While you're still awake and staring at a wall
Eyes wet and wide open
I walk through memories
Of times when you would have loved nothing more
Than to have me by your side
Tell everyone you meet
That you are in love with me

But now I am sitting alone
With my hair curled
And shoes thrown in the corner on the floor
Thinking about all the reasons
That you might not want me around anymore

***

PARACOSM

I hurt myself with imaginary scenes
Of you having the most wonderful time in secret
Without me
Of strangers scolding me from across the street
Of friends sneaking laughs behind my back
About quirks in my personality

It makes me sick to my stomach
Thinking about these cruel moments that have never been
My chest feels tight and cheeks hot
I cry until I throw up
Then stumble to my bed
To escape the nightmares created by my own head

On the smallest chance that these illusions are true
And I learned one day that the world really did hate me
And that I meant nothing to you
What would I even do

Praise my pessimistic intuition
Sleep soundly after sobbing
I told you so
To the moon
Then in the morning pick up the pieces alone

I know
I know
I know in my bones
These delusions are not real
So I try and breathe through these spiraling fantasies
Until my jaw softens
And my eyes can settle on the gardenias
Blooming outside my window

***

PARACOSM

The moon and I are quite alike
A mirror ball in the sky
That only shines when there are stars around to reflect light

Some people may feel this is a deceitful way to be
Living as a looking glass
Instead of seeking out a unique sense of authenticity

But it is difficult to find purpose in the shadows all alone
And I wish that I was someone who was more like the sun
Naturally radiant and glimmering with gold

But the thing about people like the moon and I
Is that when we receive a love
That feels extraordinary and bright
We can't help but cast that feeling back out
To anyone else who might be lost in the night

***

PARACOSM

I wish that I had the foresight
To appreciate the first time I saw snow
But how could I have known
That the magic would fade
And that the world wouldn't always feel this way
At four years old

***

PARACOSM

There are days
When I get the feeling
That if I were to fade
Into the afternoon wind
Never to be heard from again
A small part of you
Would feel relief

***

PARACOSM

I watched my friends dancing in the kitchen at a party
Laughing at the joy of it all
And I wished so badly in that moment
That I could laugh like that too

I wonder what it would feel like
To embrace joy so thoughtlessly
Effortlessly
No fear of judgement creeping up in the back of my mind

One day I hope to dance at a party
And think only about the smile of the person next to me
Instead of this irrational fear
Of being seen and misperceived

***

PARACOSM

I miss when the air was warm
When I had the freedom to go anywhere
At any time that I please

The January snow locks me in place
Forcing me to face all the feelings I hate
Under grey skies and starlight

***

PARACOSM

I hope you fall in love with peace this year
I hope you find comfort in your mornings
No matter how early or late they begin
I hope you learn to enjoy the food that makes you feel good
Both greens and chocolate ice cream

I hope you fall in love with kindness this year
I hope you find the confidence
To wear the clothes that you love
But have only shown the mirror in your room
I hope you learn to stop questioning
Both your smiles and your tears

I hope you fall in love with yourself this year
I hope you find the light within your soul
That has already guided so many back to their home
I hope you chase your dreams this year
Both relentlessly and gently

I hope you fall in love with life this year

***

PARACOSM

Today I went for a drive
To look at beautiful stone houses
With big windows
And wooden swings that sway below maple trees

I thought about how lovely it would be
To live in a home that looks like warmth
With you
And how we would eat ice cream on the porch
And dance under a chandelier

Our couch would be a soft grey
And we would watch movies
Until we accidentally fell asleep
We'd make spaghetti sauce
With basil grown on the windowsill garden
And cry together in the dark when life hit a little too hard

What a wondrous little life we would live
But these whimsical moments are just a dream in my head
When I reach the end of this life
I hope that it's your tears falling onto my wrinkled face
And your eyes in my mind
As the purest light fills me from the inside

But if that never happens
At least we laughed hand-in-hand
Once upon a time
Under my perfect imaginary sky

***

PARACOSM

These dreams that I dream
Are they manifestations of all that could be

Inspiration pulling me towards a life that I believe
Could and should and will one day be mine

Or are they distractions
Delusions keeping me from living all that my life is
And all that I will ever be

***

PARACOSM

I loved you
I loved you in all the ways that I thought you wanted
Or maybe the ways I wanted

I loved you
Until the tears I held back
As not to make you feel worse about our mutual sorrow
Ached in my cheeks and poured down my face

I couldn't love you anymore
Not in the same optimistic way that I had before
And although we have changed
We are still true to who we are at our core

I still love you
And I always will
Through winter storms and below summer stars
When I am next to you or when we are far apart

***

PARACOSM

Sometimes I run to my bed
At 8:40 PM
Just to see your face in my head
When I can't hear your voice anymore
I'll listen in my dreams
A place where you'll forever be

***

PARACOSM

The sky stayed grey today
Like it wanted to cry
But didn't know why
Or even how
The clouds moved slowly
Uneasy
Swollen with distant memories

***

Maybe I am too far gone
And the sweet words I whisper to myself in the morning
I am kind
I am brave
I am strong
Are not loud enough
To drown out the voices that have taken root in my mind
Planted by others
One at a time over the course of my life
You speak too softly to be heard
Your expectations are too high to reach
Your sorrow is to too heavy to hold
These phrases now intertwined
With every thought and decision I make
My faint affirmations do the best they can
To try and muffle the pain in my head

***

PARACOSM

I aspire to be average
I wish to become as plain as one can be
Because when you are average
You can find pockets of peace inside and unforgiving society

I want to be successful enough to avoid ridicule
Pretty enough to be treated with kindness
Smart enough to know when the right time is to speak up
While still soaring far enough below the sun
That I won't be shot down and torn apart by those who specialize
In stealing stars from the eyes of anyone who dared believe
Their dreams could come true

I wish that I was braver
So that I might see what would happen if I chased after
All that I could be
But I don't think I could handle
One more fall to the ground
So if I learn to walk as far as I can
Maybe I will see enough on my journey through this life
To satisfy this quiet itch to fly

***

PARACOSM

I am grateful to you
Because you let me sit in my sadness
Without judgement
Or expectation of peace

***

PARACOSM

February feels unbearably long
The sun starts to set at four in the afternoon
Hidden behind a silver screen of clouds across the sky
All feels frozen and hopeless when we are locked inside

Oh, but how the stars shine so bright
When the grey daylight of winter fades into darkness
The cold feels comfortable enough to settle in
And we wrap up in layers of wool
To go witness this sparkling night

The air stings my face
My nose starts to run as the snow starts to fall
It glitters in the light of your eyes
The empty grey of today has been forgotten

As we come to the end of this midnight walk
Let's pause a moment longer before going in to warm up
Pretend that the world is always this still
And that we will never run out of time
To fall in love on silent nights

***

PARACOSM

I hope you dream of something sweet tonight
I hope you dream of me

***

PARACOSM

The way I fall apart is not beautiful
Not like the death of a star
An explosion of color across the night
An ending that gives life to new constellations in the sky

I collapse into myself
Like ice caps melting into frozen waves
Destroying innocent lives with the rising tides of my rage
All while spectators question the legitimacy of my pain

And when I wake in the morning with dry and swollen eyes
There isn't some movie-like epiphany
No beautiful transformation
No fantastical new purpose found from the depths of the night

I am left with the destruction of myself
Ashes scattered across the ground
The ruins of all the bridges I have burned
When I couldn't see how else to survive

***

PARACOSM

I wish I had the grace
To walk away
When you weren't asking me
To stay anyway

***

PARACOSM

I didn't want to become stronger
I wanted to love and live life as I was

Soft

***

I'm sorry
I can't focus
Because my chapped lips have taken up my attention
It's just that I can't find my Blistex
In a purse full of wrappers and receipts
That I was too anxious to throw away in a public garbage
For some reason that I can't remember now
But felt suffocating in the moment

I'm sorry
I am too tired tonight
It's just that I didn't eat lunch
Because I had a feeling you would ask me to an early dinner
And I was right
But now I don't feel like talking
Until after the food is gone

I'm sorry
I didn't text you back last week
It's just that I didn't have the energy
To carry on a conversation right then
And I was so sure that I would feel better the next day
And the next day
And now it's an entirely new week

I'm sorry for saying sorry
But how can you not be sorry
In a world that feels like it was designed to be inconvenient
Or maybe it's just me that is the inconvenience
I'm sorry to you
And you
And you
But I am mostly sorry
That I cannot seem to figure out how to be unapologetically me

***

PARACOSM

I owe an apology to the winter
And I want to tell her before she slips away into spring
It is not you that I dislike so much as it is myself

You see
When frozen streets leave me without a way to escape
The disappointing reality around me
And I must burrow alongside the insecurities
That tumble around in my mind

I blame you
For showing me how much I dislike my life
This summer I will run away
Hide behind blooming wildflowers and willow trees
Fall asleep under the sun
To escape the life I haven't learned to love

***

Is it so wrong
That I wish to be loved
So hopelessly
So undeniably sweetly
That I'd never again question
Meaning on this earth

I know that I am supposed
To find purpose from within
And become so independently
Unshakably sure in my own skin
But sometimes
When the sky softens from afternoon to night
I wish you'd tell me
That I am what gives your world light

***

PARACOSM

I want to be the fun girl
The memorable girl
The girl that everyone wants to be around
But I am an open wound
Breaking down when the crowd gets too loud
Or when life feels too good
And I am afraid the loveliness will fade
And everyone around me will realize
That the light in me they thought they saw
Was all a façade

Maybe that's already happened
I can tell when someone finally sees through to my flaws
It's why I am ten minutes early for every date
Because I have been innocently left behind
One too many times
And I try to let it go
But instead the pain just gets buried deeper into my soul
And now I can't sleep
Or eat
Or breathe
My arms are shaking
And I can't make sense of anything

Triggered by a sign for a lost dog
How could someone let something they love
That far out of their sight
Why couldn't my friends see
That every lighthearted dig at my personality was hurting me
Maybe I can't take a joke
Or maybe I just want to feel seen

PARACOSM

What is this life for anyway
Connection
Love
Making memories that will die with me
My mind is tattered
My heart torn
How can I learn to feel alive and free once more

***

PARACOSM

All that I want is clouded by a haze of everything I should want
And if I try and fight for my authenticity
I will stand firmly alone

There are people around us have a tendency
To stand by our side only when we chase after
What they think we should be

But if you can find a way to succeed on your own
They will crawl back on their knees
And to try and learn
How you achieved the dreams they couldn't believe

***

PARACOSM

It's March and I'm broken
There's snow melting off my porch
And the sun is shining
But the air still stings
Frigid and dry
Against my tear-stained cheeks

It's March and spring starts next week
The birds have started singing
But grey skies aren't disappearing
And my hope is fading
Will I make it long enough
For summer to save me
From the sorrow of my dreams

***

PARACOSM

When you are too scared to take the first step
When you have held your breath for so long
That you have forgotten how to breathe
Under the weight of your fate
When you cannot seem to take that final leap of faith

That is when you jump
Face first into the person you have always wanted to become
There is nothing left for you
In a life where you pretend to be alright
Pleasing the people who taught you
About the meaning of transactional love

So let them go
Even if you feel alone
It will only last for a little while
And slowly you will find people
And places and talents and chances
That feel like home

***

PARACOSM

I cannot burden you with these words
So I will write them on a napkin
And then let it fly off into the breeze

But when I say that you are the one thing
That makes this life worth while
I do mean it
With every tear on my cheek
And every smile that leaves me aching for more

Of course walks in the sun
And the smell of new daisies are sweet
Moments of laughter
And a day spent by some distant sea
Are lovely in their own right

But these temporary moments of peace
Are not enough for me to endure the kind of pain
That pounds through my chest
Until the one thing that makes sense
Is for me to ruin my own being

Because why should I feel alright
When everything around me is so wrong
Except you

In your own sorrowful way
You are the one that makes me feel new
You are the quiet light that warms these endless nights
And though I can never weigh down your mind with these words
And I am sure that with further self-reflection and a little bravery
I will find more reasons to love this period of time we call life
But right now
You are the reason I have made peace with tonight

***

PARACOSM

We lay below a wisteria canopy
Eyes glazed over
Gazing up at a silvery moon

Do you think we will remember
This feeling of wonder
After the sun rises and we have parted

***

PARACOSM

When you are lost in your dreams
I hope you smile when your mind finds me

***

PARACOSM

I wish I could say I am inspired
By the daffodils that bloom
In early spring

When the air still stings
When the snow still weeps
Their golden trumpets still sing

Not in spite of frozen mornings
But in harmony
With the seasonal breeze

***

PARACOSM

Am I to have a use in this world
Does it mean anything if I do not

Would it be enough
If I left the wildflowers alone
So that they might return next spring
If I ignored the spiders in my living room corner
So that they may also have a home
If I listened more than I spoke
So that others can have a moment of release

Maybe I am here to be patient and elusive
A witness to the existence of life
Rather than some kind of epic hero
Sent by the stars to cause chaos or claim glory

Maybe all that I am in this moment
Is all that I am meant to be
And maybe that is enough

***

PARACOSM

No one else
Can feel the pain for me
I have to let go
Of the delusion
That I am somehow
Entitled to peace
I stare at the sun
Just to remember
Tears
Are a natural phenomenon

***

PARACOSM

I wish I could stop and celebrate
The small things
In extravagant ways
Like baking a lemon cake
On the first day of spring
Or throwing a party under the stars
Simply because they are shining

And I wish the world would just stop
Spinning for a moment
So I could breathe it all in
The roses
And the tea
And all of life's little wins

But the world seems to scream
There's no time
No time to slow down for joyful things
And the pressure to move on
From even the most exciting achievements
In order to continue to accomplish something— more
More
More
More
It makes me wonder
What is the point
Who is all of this for

***

PARACOSM

There is a sadness inside me
It lives deep within my soul
I lie in the grass just to feel something
Even if it is only an itch on my skin
The wildflowers dance above my head in the wind
I watch as sparrows return to their home in the trees
And wish that I could find a way to feel whole

Sometimes I think
Even if all my dreams came true
And life was joyful and loving and soft
This sadness would still be here
It's like there is a piece
That is supposed to be inside me
But it's lost

***

PARACOSM

Has the sun not risen
Does your face no longer have the strength to smile
You stare through my eyes and into my soul

The door is open my child
And the world is out there
Waiting for you to shine
Why do you choose to lock yourself inside

I think about your words
Full of frustration but kind intentions
And I know that you are right
I wish I had an answer to this question
I have wasted hours on self-reflection
Playing back every painful memory
That has made a home in my mind
Fruitless attempts to intellectualize the way that I feel
Instead of experiencing emotions shamelessly

But isn't it a shame
To feel this way
To scream and cry and laugh and sing
At least that is what I was told
To stop
Stop shouting
Wipe away your tears
Giggle don't cackle
Don't make a scene
Feel but not in a way that bothers me

Now I don't know how to be
How to live fully
Embracing all that life is and all that it means
To love and to need and to weep and to chase dreams
In a way that should come naturally

***

PARACOSM

Sometimes
The universe gives us a tiny moment
Made entirely for us
A fluorescent sunrise
A particularly gentle snowfall
A bite of perfectly ripe fruit

And if you think the heavens
Do not paint breath-taking sunsets in the sky
Just so that someone like you
Can have a quiet moment to smile
Remember that every fiber
That strings your heart together
Is a piece of this wonderous world too

So maybe today
The sparrows will chirp
Just because the world wants to hear you sing along
Or maybe the stars will send you to someone else
As a lovely reminder
A cosmic sign
That is life is worth living
That dreams do come true

***

PARACOSM

Artists always find a way
Scribbles on napkins
Monologues to mirrors
Novels is notes apps
They will sing the sweetest love songs
That only their dogs will hear
They will paint the corners of every city
If palaces will not buy their art
They will dance for pigeons in parking lots
If the stage lights go dark
My portrait will never hang in the Louvre
My words will never win a Nobel prize
But we are artists
And that gene
That extra piece
The touch of sparkle that gives us our creativity
Does not disappear because you do not approve
Because we are artists
And artists will always find a way
To leave behind pieces of their soul
In every place we stay

***

PARACOSM

If I'm being honest with myself
Sometimes
When I can feel myself shining
Just a little too bright
When I know I've struck gold
I wish for clouds
To come and filter me out
Before anyone else can tear me down

***

PARACOSM

Let's run away
To some place warm and sweet
Where we can forget the tears
That once stained our cheeks

***

PARACOSM

I'm sorry
I can't come to work today
It's seventy degrees IN APRIL
And we might not see the sun again until June

Don't fault me
Blame the Pennsylvania winter
Or climate change
Or the news

It's seventy degrees in April
And I have to soak in every last drop
Of this one wondrous and painful life
That I am slowly learning to love

***

PARACOSM

I moved to a place in my mind
Packed the best parts of me
And escaped to an infinite dream

Where I lived everywhere and no where
Did everything and nothing
And I did it all with you

We danced in Paris
Laughed in Milan
And sang to the Aurora Borealis

We lived a dream
In my fantasies
Until I realized that's all it was

I gave everything
To the story in my mind
Instead of the life before my eyes

So this is to a new beginning
And actually saying the word *Hello*
Instead of letting you go

***

PARACOSM

I sit under a tree
Try to breathe
But these thoughts of everything that's ever hurt
And everything that ever could burn
Are drowning my mind in a cloud of make-believe and lies

Close your eyes
Breathe
In, two, three, four
Hold
Out, two, three, four

Open your eyes
What are five things you can see
The leaves are green
A dragon fly resting on a daisy
The mascara that's dripped onto my knee
A fence in the distance
Purple wildflowers wilting

Four things you can feel
An unreleasable tightness in my forehead
My shirt shaking in the breeze
The warmth of the sun on my cheeks
Shoes too tight around my feet

Breathe

Three things you can hear
Two sparrows singing softly overhead
My heart racing inside my neck
The faded hum of a lawn mower down the street

PARACOSM

Two things you can smell
The distinct scent of grass in mid-spring
The remnants of the perfume
I optimistically sprayed this morning

Breathe

One thing you can taste
The dryness in my mouth is burning

Am I out of my mind
I'll try again
Five things I can see
Five things I can see
Five things
I can't see
My eyes are now blurry
I wish I knew how to love the moment
Instead of living inside the pain of memories long past
And worries of an unknown future
But I am now too far away
From who I once was
To know enough about who I am
To remember what it means
To see the present so clearly

***

PARACOSM

What an unfair burden I have placed onto myself
To dream of a life so sweet
Imagine the most beautiful future memories
When time and time again
These expectations for a marvelous reality
Turn out to be exceptionally average in every way
And if I had waited for these tender moments
To play out naturally
Maybe I would be living out my life a little more gratefully

***

PARACOSM

We laid under the hemlock trees
Watched as their leaves danced in the breeze
But I knew when your smile widened
And your eyes brightened
It was not because I made you feel free
And you'll never think of me
When you see a hemlock tree

***

PARACOSM

Hold on for one hour more
For me
If you can sit with this pain
For one more hour
I promise the world
Won't hurt so much anymore
When the tears dry
Your eyes might burn
Your cheeks will be sore
And in one hour's time
It won't feel alright
But it will feel a little lighter
Just a tiny bit brighter

And even if it doesn't
I'll have held you for an hour more
Then I'll ask you to give me another
Because I need you now
Like I have never needed anyone before
I need you right here
Right now
Just as you are
A mess on the floor
For one more hour
And then another hour more

PARACOSM

Then when you wake tomorrow
Your head still heavy
Your mouth still dry
I'll bring you a glass of water
And together we can cry
About how we made it another eight hours
And it wasn't so bad
Then we will laugh together
Until we remember we were sad

So please just give me one hour more

***

PARACOSM

You are a sight for sore eyes
Eyes that have cried through the night
Now swollen and dry
Squinting in the morning sky
Softened again by your smile and sighs

***

PARACOSM

Come and sing with me
Out in first storm of spring
Dance in the rain
Until our song turns to screams
And no one else will see
The tears on our cheeks
When we release the pain
Of suffocated dreams

***

How is it that I have become the enemy in this scene
That my need to please and appease
Has somehow made me a master of manipulation
When I have not been allowed to learn
Any other way to be

Love is conditional
Don't pretend like it's not
And I am only a human
I cannot ignore my need to feel like I belong
Like I am loved

If I don't keep you happy
You lock me outside the garden gates
And if I have to listen to your insults and screams one more time
I am afraid that my mind might break
Like the porcelain plates you throw past my face
When you yell that I have nothing to cry about

I will sink into myself in private
And keep a soft smile on my face
While the core of who I am burns to ash
Because time and time again I have been shown
That to get what I need
To survive in a world where gentle acceptance is a scarcity
I have to become the version of me
That you want to see

***

PARACOSM

Sometimes
You must protect your peace
And sometimes
You must go to war for it

***

PARACOSM

I gave all my love
But in all the wrong ways
I hope you remember my gentle intentions
Instead of my mistakes

***

PARACOSM

It is May
And there are fresh tulips on the table
Lemon cake in the oven
And your smile is shining in my eyes

The air is light
And for the first time in a while
I have forgotten all of my sorrows
And the is no place else in this world I'd rather be

***

PARACOSM

We were supposed to be watching the moon
But I spent the whole night with my eyes on you

***

PARACOSM

It's late spring
And the flowers smell so sweet
I almost forget that I am
Hopelessly wandering below the trees

It's as if I have entered some kind of
In between reality and dream
How can world with so much pain
Smell of a gentle floral breeze

***

I wish that I loved you better when I had the chance
Go back in time
So I could hold your hand
When it slid out of your pocket
And hung by your side
Grab your face
Kiss it one more time

I would say that
I hope you know that I love you
More than I ever dreamed someone could
Love another person
But I don't think you do
And it's my fault for not saying enough
Not doing enough

Not because you weren't enough
But because I couldn't get out of my own mind
Paralyzed by the thought
That one day you'd leave me behind
For something grander
Someone cooler
Someone altogether better than I could ever be
I have lost my heart
Because of my own insecurities

***

PARACOSM

Will you lay with me
Stay with me
In my garden of dreams

Your hand resting on mine
While peonies dance in the breeze

Will you wait with me
Play with me
Until the stars fade above the trees

Your eyes locked into mine
While the fallen leaves burry our feet

Will you stay with me
Remain with me
Even after the rains wash our bodies away

Your life intertwined with mine
Long after the world forgets we were alive

**

PARACOSM

I believe that you alone
Are the reason the sky blushes
Before fading into the night

***

PARACOSM

I am getting better and it hurts
It hurts so much to grow
And watch a version of yourself disappear while you heal
It hurts to watch people you love grow in different directions
And to know that I can never go back to who I was
Because I know better now
I don't think we talk enough about the pain of healing
I know that without growth
We wilt
But it doesn't mean that I don't miss
All the ways I bloomed before
In spite of storms
Not because of them

***

PARACOSM

There are days
When I feel so sensibly lucky to be me

And then there are todays
When my mind becomes
An inconsolable wreckage of self-loathing
Dreaming about what might have been
Or what could only be if—

I hope to find some sort of balance
Between dreams and peace
Or at least a way to accept pain graciously

***

PARACOSM

I am allowed to leave
People and places and jobs
That make me feel unworthy

I am allowed to leave
When you tell me
I should just be grateful things aren't worse

When you tell me
That I am too sensitive
After calling attention to the ways I have been hurt

But I am not an inconvenience
And I don't have to stay around people
Who make me feel small

I am worthy of a life
That makes me feel
Like I can have it all

***

PARACOSM

I am sorry for the time that I couldn't be what you needed
It's just that I am still learning
It is okay to ask for help when you need it
That it is okay to be human

***

PARACOSM

I go for a walk
To get lost in my mind
Twist and turn
Through thoughts I don't like
Until the trees and the breeze
Whisper
It will all be alright
And my tears dry under the sunlight

***

PARACOSM

I promise you
It is alright if you had to hide away
From everything and everyone for a little while
Turn off all the lights
So you felt safe enough to cry
And sort through the terrifying thoughts in your mind

Sometimes you can't reach out and ask for help
Because you don't yet have words
To describe all the hurt and emotions trapped inside
Feeling is not the same as healing
And it is okay if you need some time
To sit with your sadness
Before relearning how to live your life

***

June is for flowers so fresh
They leave you smelling earthy and sweet
June is for dancing
June is for joy
June is for falling in love
With birds learning to sing
Go lay in the light under the trees
And listen to the laugh
Of someone who makes you feel free
Because it's the first day of June
And June is for living your daydreams

***

PARACOSM

I think often about a sailboat
I drew when I was eight or nine years old
I have no idea where this picture now lives
Likely shriveled and stained in a landfill
Below plastic bags and scrap metal

In my mind
This sailboat was the most miraculous work of art
I have ever created
I remember a distinct sense of pride
When I unveiled my piest de resistance
Sketched on a bumpy pink desk
To my parents
Their friends
And my cat

Mechanical pencil on printer paper
Emma
2003

In truth
I don't really know if this scribble was a master piece
Or just magic in my eight-year-old mind
I also don't know when I stopped creating regularly
Off and on I still pick up a pen or paint brush
But nothing I have ever sketched since
Has compared to that sailboat in my head

PARACOSM

Maybe I stopped because people I met
Told me that I make a better realist than artist
And that I should focus my time
On endeavors that would help seal my seat
At a prestigious university
Followed by a glorious career
In some presently un-nameable field
A mortgage
Annual trip to the sea
And eventually a retirement where I would finally have the time
To live out my delusional artistic fantasies

Or maybe I just decided
That I'd rather spend my time
Dancing around with other interests
Like writing
Or perfecting chocolate chip cookie recipes
Or climbing trees

I really don't know the answer
As to why I let my pencils and paper disintegrate
With the dust in my closet
But I do know
That I loved that sailboat
And at one time
I loved to sing
And run
And swim
And fail at new things
And I really believed
That I could do anything I wanted with my life
Maybe that thought is still true
Deep down inside the hollows of my soul
I know that life is full of endless potential
And castaway dreams have a way of floating back to me
Maybe that sailboat was a masterpiece

PARACOSM

Or maybe it was nothing more than a memory
I just hope that one day
I find the courage to shamelessly try and become
All that I might be

***

PARACOSM

I hope you find a way
To feel like yourself again one day

***

What have I done
Oh what have I done with my one life
I have wished every wonderful and heartbreaking moment away
Hoping that it could be different
That I could be different
Lost in dreams of all that could be
I am afraid that I have missed
What could have been the best moments I will ever get
I solemnly swear to love all that is to come
This gift that it is to be
To experience beauty and joy and tragedy
Please don't let the best have passed me by
I promise now
That I will love this life

***

PARACOSM

I can feel myself slipping into a new version of myself
A lighter version of myself
A me that loves to try new things again
And spend late nights with friends again

A version of myself
That still cries below the trees at midnight
Asking why it feels so painful to be alive
But now when the sun rises
I am able to remember the love and laughter and joy
That also fills my life

I hope this new me
Enters the world gracefully
That I won't be afraid to dance under the stars
Or sing soft melodies

I hope this new me is kind to people who try and tear me down
That I don't dwell on bitter words from the people
Who think they know me better than I know myself
Words that are really aimed at their own insecurities

I hope that I remember life is meant to be lived
And how important it is to tell people how you really feel
Thoughtfully and truthfully
Not to water down love or ignore the anger in my chest
For the sake of keeping a false sense of peace

I hope that I can find the courage to lie back and float
When waves of sorrow about all that I cannot control
Try to drown my mind with self-loathing and doubt

PARACOSM

There are times in life when we can feel ourselves changing
Moments that send an unmistakable feeling through our minds
That we will never be the same again
And I can feel this gradual transformation
Starting to glow from the inside of my soul
I hope this new version of me
Leads to an era of peace

***

PARACOSM

What if I have fallen in love with the rain
And how when it falls from the sky
I am overcome by an urge to run

Lost in a storm I finally feel something
A reminder that I am alive washes over me
A needed moment of emotion
When I am usually content with feeling numb

Maybe I don't know what it means to feel at peace
I can't quite remember what happiness means

***

PARACOSM

Is it so wrong of me
To always want a warm breeze
For every day to feel
Like the first day of summer
And always pick the ripest peach

The world will tell you
To live each day like it is your last
And in the same breath
Scold you to lower your expectations
Appreciate pain
Because sorrow teaches you
How wonderful it is feel to love by contrast

But I have cried more than most in a lifetime
And I am tired of submitting to second best
I don't think it is wrong for me
To want my joy to last

***

PARACOSM

I want to remember this moment
Sitting on the porch
Watching the rain fall steady on one side
And the sun set below the mountains on the other
An orange glow frames your smile
And my mind feels light

When I play back my life each night
And I think about every time that I cried
I want to think about this moment instead
Chase more memories like these
Where I smile
And think about nothing but this moment in my life

***

PARACOSM

I blink three times
And dance in sunshine
Listen to the secrets
Only whispered on beaches
Let go of every melodramatic tear
That watered my make believe nightmares
The bliss begins
Now that summer has warmed my skin

***

PARACOSM

I will love you
For as long as you will let me
And even then
I am not so sure I would stop

***

PARACOSM

All I can think about
Are the moments we didn't get
The afternoon walks we missed
The late-night whispers that were silenced
We were supposed to be the very definition of destiny
But the stars still have yet to align
So we watch them glitter through the night
Stealing time while the makers and creators of fate
Are distracted by the illusions of light across their skies

***

PARACOSM

Let me cry alone
Let the summer storm drown out my tears
Let me weep below the drooping willow
Let no one catch wind of my fears

Let me cry alone
Let lightning strike my memory
Let my regrets overflow
While I figure out how you left me
To sit and cry alone

***

I turned twenty-six today
Twenty-six feels like some sort of sentence
In a place that hates old women
I am not old
You know this
I know this too
But the single grey hair I found last month says different
The filtered faces on my screen say different
The health insurance company says different
My time is slipping away
The courts overturned Roe v. Wade
All in the same week
I should be celebrating this wonderful one-time existence
Instead I play a melancholy song
And watch the daisies wilt in the summer sun
We are finite things
Born only to die
I can't help but feel grateful yet devastated
To be alive

***

PARACOSM

I just want to be loved
In the same way a daisy wants to feel the sun
And I don't think that is selfish or wrong

***

PARACOSM

I'll offer you my most sincere
It will all be alright
Because what else do I say
When we both know
It will never feel okay
At least not in the same way-
That you will come out of this changed
And *alright* has become
A relative phrase
There can't be such a force as fate
What have we done
To deserve irreversible pain

***

PARACOSM

I could walk home
But when the sun is bright
And the air is warm
How can I leave this dream
Playing out in real time

***

PARACOSM

Let's lay out under the sun
Pretend like we haven't lived through our past
Let's play make-believe with transient clouds
Forget about a future that never had a chance
Let's give up on shooting stars and dandelion dreams
A wish can't save us
No matter how many times we whisper *please*
Let's just lay out under the sun
Imagine we can stay forever young

***

July
Sweet red cherries
Summer's breeze
Too hot to overthink
July is for the hopelessly in love
July is for me

***

PARACOSM

I would like to say
That I live for the small moments
For the spaces and places
That bring a smile across my cheeks
The minutes that are so beautifully all consuming
That I don't have a chance to overthink
About how leaving behind this soon to be memory
Will send me back to the tear-stained reality of life

Are these fleeting moments of mindless bliss
Worth the return to a despair
Which has permeated my fragmented soul so deeply
I can't comprehend how to stay soft
How to stay me
Under the weight of this sorrow

That is a question I firmly believe
I will never have an answer to
For I have loved deeply
And laughed loudly
And sang sweetly
And lived freely
But behind every joyful scene
Is the certainty
That this indescribable grief will once again take over me

***

PARACOSM

I hope you remember me fondly
I hope you smile when you think of my flaws
And how hard I tried to overcome
All that I could not control

I hope you know that I loved you
Even when I couldn't do anything
Other than cry on the floor
And complain about the unfairness of it all

I hope you still love me
When you think of those distant memories
I hope you still see me through kind eyes
And know I gave you the best of my soul

***

PARACOSM

If you have an inclination
A pique of interest
A feeling that something is meant for you

Chase it with everything you have
Don't stop to breathe
Don't ask what others think

Take that glimmer of a gift
And go as fast as you can
As far as the universe will allow

You will be amazed at the places you see
When you finally give yourself permission
To run free

***

PARACOSM

I lost myself to the anger that took root in my mind
At a time when I could not understand
That pain is not a temporary state of being
But a life-long companion

I did not know that rage must be embraced as a warning
Stemming from a place of self-love
Before it consumes every single last one of my thoughts

I am sorry for the person I was
When my anger became a weapon
Instead of a moment of self-refection

An indication that I needed to open myself to love
Instead of running away
To sulk alone in the shadows of desperation

***

PARACOSM

Could you love every version of me
Weepy and full of self-pity
Or even worse
Glowing and proud of who I am
Head over heels in love
Or frantic and searching for comfort

Is that fair for me to ask
Is that a reasonable kind of love to want
I know that I could love you
Through every phase of the moon
Do you think you could love me like that too

***

I dance with the dandelion seeds
That swirl through a summer breeze
Wishes and dreams carried by the wind
That I send up to the sky
In hopes that one day
They will remember my smile
And bring me back to life

***

PARACOSM

I need to sit in my sorrow
Just for a little while longer
I appreciate your kindness
Sweet words of encouragement
Suggestions and solutions to problems
That at this time I don't have the strength to overcome

Right now I need to lie on the floor in this sadness
My mind is fractured
From the weight of my feelings
And all I can hear in my head
Is the echo of hurtful words and distant memories
But your hand in mine is enough comfort to know
It will all be okay in the end

***

PARACOSM

I am overcome with grief
For the person I might have been
Had I not allowed the words of skeptics and naysayers
To build a home in my head

***

PARACOSM

Whether dreams are stolen, killed, or self-immolated
Is neither here nor there

What matters most
Is this right now
This one life I have to live

And though I am not happy
I am not as unhappy as I used to be

Does that mean I don't still dream

Of course not

But I am trying to learn
How to make peace with reality

***

PARACOSM

The dog days of summer
The Sunday of seasons
The warmth of the trees
The glow of the evenings

August
Will you promise me to slow down
If I swear to savor every drop of you

***

PARACOSM

I was never more myself
Then when I was singing in the car with you
Off-key to pop radio tunes
Going anywhere that looked like an adventurous place
To capture memories on camera
And talk for hours about everything and nothing

We should be laughing on a beach today
About imaginary plans for taking over the world
About mistakes we made when we were young
And obscure names given to the ice cream flavors at the store on the boardwalk

We should be crying together in my room tonight
About the things we wanted to do but could not
About the boys who broke our hearts without a second thought
And the unfairness of the circumstances that hold us back from our dreams

We should be friends today
And words that were or weren't exchanged shouldn't matter
Because sometimes you meet another soul
That burns light in the same shades as you
And you don't need to speak to know
That they understand you in a way
That is beautifully impossible to describe

I hope you still sing in the car
And bake cookies for the people you love
I hope when you sit on the edge of a mountain peak
After a long hike through the woods
You think of me
And know that I am lying under the sun
Thinking of you too

***

PARACOSM

Lay with me
Under this golden breeze
Lock your fingers in mine
While we laugh below a rose-colored sky
Leave behind all your doubts
Until the daisies chain us to the ground

***

PARACOSM

I think that everyone else
Must know what I know
Love what I love
See what I see
And that they all have a way
Of doing it all so much better than me

But the truth is
That no one else has lived what I have lived
Feels what I feel
Dreams what I dream

These people I see
Who seem to be altogether more perfect than me
Are lovely
Wonderously
And beautifully themselves

Just like I am
Lovely
Wonderously
And beautifully me

We are all chasing after our own fantasies
We all fall and second guess our choices
Insecure in what it is to be human

On the days when you feel alone
Behind
And as though you couldn't possibly be enough
Please remember
That you are lovely
And wonderous
And beautiful too

***

PARACOSM

On a soft September night
I finally feel a wave of peace wash over the tension in my jaw
My skin feels warm against the breeze
And it glows slightly pink from a summer spent below the sun

I rest my eyes under a tree
Memorizing how sweet the wildflowers sing
And imagining what this green canopy
Will look like in three weeks
A blush of orange and red below a golden autumn sun

I feel grounded in this place between memories and daydreams
Is this what it means to live in the moment
To stop and smell the roses
To find a way to be grateful for what is
Instead of losing myself in all that could be or has been

***

PARACOSM

I believe that if there was a reason
I was placed on this earth
It was to take long beautiful walks
And listen to the wildflowers sing

***

PARACOSM

I finally understand
How the daisies release
Petals grown
Through a summer of love

When winter frost
Settles below the trees
They do not fear that their return
Has not been promised by the sun

They do not mourn
The life they once loved
They let go
Because they must

There is nothing else left to do
But become dust
Rest while the world
Mourns their loss

And when warm light stirs their sleep
From an uncertain slumber
They will remember how to dance once more
While the sparrows sing

***

PARACOSM

And in the silence between your sorrowful dreams
May your heart feel a moment of peace

***

PARACOSM

Made in the USA
Coppell, TX
03 February 2024